HEAR MY CRIES

THE STREET JAZZ & GHETTO BLUES OF AN ONLY CHILD

Chris Slaughter

Published by Chris Slaughter

Black Alchemist Press, Ink.
Publishing Consulting Services

Black Alchemist Press, Inc.
Puslishing Consulting Services
PO Box 110569
Jamaica, NY 11411-0569
718.525.0812 718.369.7422
646.843.6677 fax 718.499.7236
www.blackalchemistpress.com

Chris Slaughter
240 Moffat St. #3R
Brooklyn, NY 11207 (718)452-3391

LIBRARY OF CONGRESS
CATALOGING-IN-PUBLICATION DATA
Slaughter, Chris
Library of Congress Card Number: 00-106222
        Hear My Cries
        I. Poetry. I. African-American fiction
        II. Auto-biographical Fiction II. Social Issues
ISBN 0-9671082-3-3

Cover design by Phillip Shung
Cover layout by Black Alchemist Press, Ink.

The Geshen cafe
on 5th Bt. 130th & 131st.
on 9/27/00 8:30PM

To: "Dustay"

Copy Written by Heart
&
Published by Soul.

*Thanks for the
Support Sister

Hope you

Hear My Cries

Chris Sly*

Acknowledgments

The most important woman in my life, my mom, Vanessa Slaughter. Father, Christopher Shannon. Aunt Rita, Aunt Flo, Aunt Jenette, tee-tee, Antoine. Aunts: Mary, Sally and Louise. My Josephine, Grand Dad Shannon, little sis Tiesha, Aunt Deborah, you helped speed this book into progress. Aunt's Nancine & Dez, My Militant Poets: Randy Angus and lucano Atilola Ishaka, thanks for giving me two more right hands. To the woman who hurt me in the past, thanks for unblindfolding me. Big thanks goes to a teacher I was fortunate to meet in the High School of Transit Tech, the late DR. Walker, thanks for noticing my writing. Tie, Pooh bear, Rahn and Chester, my first real peoples. Worm-(Mike) Jamie and Devon, Mag-(Lionel), Black-(Demeko), Jerry, Breeze-(Omar) Teroy-(Tyrese) D-Rock- (David) and Fat Cat-(Nakia). Gerren Liles who I met On The Road to Damascus. Messiah, one of the real poets out there. Essence; my good luck charm. To my caus. Afreka, thanks for getting me through those unbearable nights. My Latino Southern Girl Kim. Norma my friend for life. Pamela, the ideal woman, Parker, My man poop-(Milan), Chevon, Kamel, Fortez, Man, all my customers-Barber shop. Pitch Black (Jean, Doe, Shane, zah and Devious). Snyp and Tie, Jason the illest artist ever. THE late Donald Goines for inspiring me to write more. The late 2 Pac Shakur for helping me writing from the heart, its all I know how to do now. Kool G Rap, Rakim, Canibus, the Roots. And to Common Sense, you're right ; One day it will all make sense. And last but not least Marléna Gasper, Thanks for working with me. Self publishing a book was always one of my dreams. Black Alchemist Press, Ink. will definitely be a big name some day.

R.I.P

Tyrone max - Things just aint the same here without you son, and oh yeah! I kept my promise.

Shakiecia Faussett - I know you would've been leading the league in scoring,
you probably up there running the point for GOD!

Damien Bonito - I can't drive down Halsey St. without being thrown back
to that night of SEPT. 16, RAIN!

Auntie Dora - the craziest woman to ever touch the grounds of Connecticut. the boldest, funniest and most spontaneous person I ever met.
"If you've ever met her, you love her".

Sean Jenkins - One of the strongest guys I ever knew. You kept a sense of humor and
maintained a smile in the hardest of times.
I admired your strength. I hope you like the poem I wrote for you.
Lowell Nicholas (low-G)- Crazy, funny, outgoing and out spoken. He could make
you laugh till you cry. One of the funniest guys I every met, but always handled
his business. definitely a guy worth knowing.

Calvin Holcombe - T o describe Calvin is almost unthinkable. he was the guy you
think would leave here of old age. kind, funny, and never into anything undestructive.
The type of friend you'd only see in movies.... IDEAL.

CRADLE OF CONTENTS

ACKNOWLEDGMENTS
R.I.P

11	ONLY CHILD
14	DEAR GHETTO
15	ONCE LOVED
17	HAIKU
18	ENGAGEMENT
19	THE BIGGEST MISTAKE EVER TOLD
21	STREET JAZZ GHETTO BLUES
24	BLIND VIEWS OF AWARENESS
26	COLD AND WINDY CLICHÉ'S
	(of my essence)
28	LOST IN THE RAIN
30	CARDIAC
32	HEARTBREAK
34	EXPRESSIONS
35	WHEN HOPE DIES
38	TEARS IN THE RAIN
40	GHETTO GOSPEL
43	HEAR MY CRIES
46	DEAR LOVE

47　HAIKU
49　THE REALEST SHIT I EVER WROTE
51　THE UNTITLED TITLE
53　STAY... NO LEAVE
55　ALLEY CAT
57　THE 19th LETTER
60　FRIENDS
63　ROSE IN THE SNOW
65　PROSPECT PARK
66　BLACKOUT
69　BROOKLYN STATE OF MIND
72　I THOUGHT I WAS OVER YOU
74　STEP FORWARD STEP BEHIND
76　HAIKU
77　FROM THE HEART TO MY ESSENCE
79　MOVED ON
80　ANGELS
81　AMERICA OFF LINE
83　SURVIVE TO DIE
84　CANCEROUS THOUGHTS
86　A SUICIDE NOTE
87　UMBILICAL SLANG

MONOLOGUES
91　NO ONE UNDER STANDS
93　CHANGING

THE STREET JAZZ & GHETTO BLUES OF A SEMI-BASTARD CHILD

THE ONLY CHILD

Look into my eyes and read my book,
Embraced this book that is copy written by my heart,
and published by my soul,
casting vigorous portraits
That sunbathe on park benches.

My life is written in a font that you can only read
when your hat is to the back
Sitting on a graffiti covered train-
With the lights blinking,
Sitting next to a kid who is an only child
acting as your dictionary to nocturnal words,
Cause you can't possibly understand me
If you have brothers and sisters,

I am the only child,
Afraid of the dark,
Forced to create sporadic images,
left alone to single handedly think,
Now I do my best writing in the dark with black ink...

Got in trouble in school for excessive talking cause I had
No kids to speak to at home,
Had a love for art,
drew picture after picture and wrote
Poem after poem...
Narrating the streets from my third
Floor window,

older cats would lead women to the park;
two finger ring on the right
with a woman clinging to his left,
Thinking, that heavy early 80's shit
lost its strength when it hit the wind
.....trying their hardest to imitate goldie
And super fly,

light headed,
corner of my eye
uncle rolls weed on an old record cover,
razor blade to separate the seeds,
agony tightly rolled between bamboo paper,
Casting misery from his nostrils,
Closing his eyes, surrounded by disappearing thoughts
of his fourth daughter.

An only child,
suffocated by weed smoke,
Drowning in booze,
I had one mom, half a pops,
two uncles and no rules,
I left myself clues,
Take the "L" train to wilson ave.
Or the "J" train to chauncey st.
A child forced to walk a mile in a man's shoes,

In some crazy way I was similar to that kid from
sixth sense,
... I've seen dead people....
But they were alive,
Roaming the streets abroad,

pants hanging so low it
Altered their stride,
In a cemetery of thought I buried them in my writing,
Creating imagery of casket- like poetry,

born alone die alone,
mommy can't have no more kids,
besides I was just a mistake anyway,
Too deep for words yet still...I write,

but it's too late and I'm here now,
L   I   F   E ! I'm up all in it,
And you can burn this book
if you ever catch me in an abortion clinic,

The hardships and the perpetual cries
I lived amongst it,
I got my mothers name across my stomach,
And the pain of my tattoo,
couldn't compare to the pain
She felt when I was coming,
Me and mom felt pain
but daddy felt no pain
When he was... coming,
And why the fuck he lied
On all the christmas's when he said he was
... coming ?

Popa was a rolling stone,
where ever he laid his dick was his home,
And when he lied, all he left us was alone

DEAR GHETTO,

Have you forsaken us? Your breath seeps through every crack and crevice making my people extinct. When you exhale, babies born in the ghetto lie stillborn before birth, being conceived already dead, Making the womb of life into an open casket. You inject poison into the veins of our side streets, Blow smoke through the avenue of our minds, And corrupt every other block with a liquor store. You made religion into a hypocritical house that people call church, unknowingly praying to you, Subconsciously hoping they brake the shackles Of their motivational deficiency. You got us negroes stugglin, hustlin, throwing up The fist of black power with diamonds surroundin Our fingers . . . . . . what type of shit is that. You nonchalant inconsiderate mother....you just don't get it do you? You have children in every borough, Grandchildren in every room, sleeping on crowded mattresses, While the mothers out giving head just to get her hair done. At this point you're probably planning on writing me back in bullet holes, putting me in a casket like envelope, with blood covering the paper.

PS that's why I didn't put a return address on the envelope

ONCE LOVED

Do angels lose their wings..
If the beauty of their feathers are revealed ?
I've once seen heaven in her eyes,

I often held her close enough
 to smell eternal sweetness
In the nectars that indulged her tongue,
Feeling intimidated by darkness,
Until I kissed her lips
With my eyes closed,

those eyes... those eyes
Had me acting as a junkie,
Carrying around different pictures
in every pocket................
Even when I had no pockets,

Her scent... her scent
Spiraled around inside of my nose,
Teasing the strength of my knees,
Forcing me to sit down
each time she stood before me,

She had a smile that made god
Admire his work.
Framing prisms of sunshine
That grew from her eyes the minute

She awakened at dawn,

I sometimes didn't listen,
words often bore me,
I was interested in the expressions
that posed in the background
Of her reactions,

Then suddenly it hit me....
I couldn't love her more if I tried,
Her beauty just brings
Pleasure to my eyes,
I just can't seem to get over being...... once loved

Haiku

If love is a house
I'm homeless on the cold streets
wrapped in memories

ENGAGEMENT

We spoke the same languages with different accents,
we came from the same universe yet fabricated in different
worlds, Her blunted high mixed with my natural high
brought confusion to everyday sound, third listeners couldn't
understand our slang dialect with just a touch of English.

We brought a liberating harmony to ghetto ear
drums, when we argued, we screamed in silent noise that
caused alley cats to cry and beg for us to make up.

We had different organs that didn't
compliment, yet still gave each other mental orgasms,
our bodies never touched, our words were monogamous with
phone operators, before visually touching dilated pupils.

We became close enough to experience each other's
breath in different boroughs, our kisses were wet enough to
drown thoughts and create beaches with no sand.

Whenever in disagreement we sought a doctor by the
name of Donald Goines. he brought our ghettos together
and made sense of our conflicting tensions,
we then applied non-fictional theories to his wise words,
which erected our wisdom of each other's poverty stricken
streets.

We never met on the same block, but something
happened that never happened before, Two avenues connect-
ing on a dead end street.

THE BIGGEST MISTAKE EVER TOLD

Glamorous, elegant and stunning she was,
Like a view of the ocean on a moon lit night she was,
Like african art work singing over a village of
Broken spirits she was,
Mine..... she was,

Sunshine dances in rain drops just to fall in her
Hair on cloudy days,
Humming unreleased melodies of Billie Holiday
In soprano slang,

Saxophones in the dark describes her voice,
With soft sounds of violin jazz notes
mingling in the background of
Spoken word alto jive,

The biggest mistake ever told
consisted of no words,
Just tears that fell onto guitar strings
and strummed submissive
rhythmic sounds of heartbreak,

Making love in candle lit rooms,
Erotic shadows bending
into positions of musical
Orchestrations of
. . . . .love making,

I let something go that was never truly mine,
I borrowed another man's love........

The biggest mistake ever told
Was him not telling her how....

Glamorous , elegant and stunning she was,

STREET JAZZ / GHETTO BLUES

I'm from where green money became extinct,
> And welfare, food stamps, and Medicaid gave birth
>> to children by the minute.
Brand name shoes teased me from store front windows,
> Hoping to one day shelter my toes,
> And when the winter hit: I could see my breath,
>> feeling exceedingly cold,
> My shoes had cheap soles.
> No heat and hot water, one parent performed 2 roles,
> Dope corrupted my uncle; at the dinner table I've
>> seen him doze.
I grew my first chest hair when my grandmoms died,
>> my second heart caught a stroke, my mind ran into a
>>> dark corner of her room to hide.
> If I ever told you I never cried,
> I lied-
>> a piece of her still lives in me.
Some say I was fashioned from my mother,
> from the womb I upset my parents, and cried to a
>> young mother peeved,
> I say I was caste from the sky swathed in turbans,
>> shattering the concrete screaming, I believe!
> Smiling to the most high with
>> Omega branded on my sleeves,
> Angels whispering, making threats to my heart,
>> demanding me to achieve.
I watched my cousin locked up most of his life,
> Only his daughters know where his soul is.

Two seeds planted,
      concrete surrounds two fatherless roses.
I scream, "let my people free" speaking in piercing
      tongues of a ghetto moses.
Satan injects ugliness in our veins
      and hate through our noses.

Young girl overly developed
      hopping in & out of exotic foreign cars.
Young girl overly developed
      removing her clothes in clubs & bars.
Young girl overly developed
      shattered mentally chasing ghetto stars.
Older man attracts younger girl
      with war stories and battle scars.

I write street jazz and ghetto blues,
      Corruption of my habit narrated through the mis
      conceptions and the ignorance of the news.
      Words are misconstrued
      Through the ears of fools,
      You can't pawn my words; Just rock these jewels,
I write street jazz and ghetto blues.

Tell me... how could I be a chip off the old block when my
      old block had no chips?
      My block had hustlers, drugs and full clips.
      Pissy mattresses for handsprings and back flips.
      Old men stood on the corner
      hissin at a young ass and firm tits.
Remember this; scaly games shoot for the box and pot,
      no more games kids tote guns and smoke pot.

Seen my man die / block party /a few shots,
we used to shoot the hands bloody nose a few knots.
No more hands /gun cocked in pine box.
 Judge my attitude, my life is hard knocks,
my best friend turned blood,
        got locked for selling rocks,
who told the story best but C. Wallace and 2Pac.

You see I was raised on the streets
            did best of what I had,
I can't change him being my biological,
            I had no dad.
At first cursed my birth, it drove me more than mad,
he should've pulled out
            and busted his nut on a rag....dag!

BLIND VIEWS OF AWARENESS

Past and present obstacles
Puzzle my life together
Placing pieces that don't fit.
My present was a present,
  destined for perfection crumbling to pieces
Before my very eyes,

My past eclipses with my present

Torn between thin lines of
  shattered walks
Through climaxing dreams
        of slippery paths,

Wanting my present to un blindfold my past
From around my eyes,
Reversing my blindness of perception,

In the cross roads of life,
Driving in reverse with
My present beside me,
Crashing into the past
Making my present a casualty of love,

Forcing tears of inner screams
With confusion soaked
In the moisture of my tongue.
Caught up in some talk show shit,

television off
eyes glued to
The screen wondering
 what else the fuck could happen?

The inevitable french kissing
         My yesterdays ,
Spelling my destiny in braille across stucco walls,
Confusing the finger tips of
My blind inner self,
         Relying solely on memory.

Common sense guides me back to
         Reality,
Waking me up from
A dream of time rewinding
         Uncontrollably,
Forcing counter clock wise decisions
 upon my present,
With audacity itself
Daring me to endure my past.

COLD AND WINDY CLICHÉS
(of my essence)

It was a hot summer day in the month of July
when I first felt this breeze,
It came across so innocently cool
she dried up my tears of loneliness.

This breeze was peaceful enough
to dry all humidity surrounding my being,
It brought with it cliché's
that blew through the tree's; that
Were deep rooted in the untainted soils of my heart.

The clichés were much deeper than
I Love You and I Need You,
They sank deep into the pores of my skin,
and when her wind blew onto my Essence,
Her clichés would sing their way into my soul.

Trapped in her wind were rose petals,
with tulip shaped silhouettes,
That danced between darkness and light
flirting with gardens that prayed
to embrace her redolence.

Who would have ever imagined with this wind
came emotional tornadoes,
And visions of angels
with broken halos and tattooed wings.

This wind had unforgotten stones
from her former atmosphere
that taught me lessons,
not to take off my jacket to ever windy cliché
That promised me serenity.

Her wind became cold,
so cold in fact it could freeze hell
and make it snow there,
She took on the form of an angel in flight,
with illusions of logic
that played love stories in-between blinks.

Cookies and cream clichés danced on my tongue
with butter pecan shoes,
Teasing my taste buds with calories of love.......
Have you ever kissed love?
Well I've tasted infatuation with caramel coated thoughts
and chocolate covered dreams.

I walked around with my emotions on my sleeve
forced to believe, that if you left,
my pride and sanity would leave,
unabling me to physically breath,
But I am still breathing .... No more Windy days

LOST IN THE RAIN

Eyes close, death calls
I hear moans, long distance thoughts
from the voice that killed my boy
I still be dialing 771-8770
line disconnected
Death called,
he answered
Silent dialtones
tears soak my beard

I had nothing to do with this poem. . .
Crying old photos
that got stuck under my eyelids making it hard
For me to drive . . . so I crashed into your memories,

My whole world fell into darkness, envisioning
Your son with two halos suspended above him,
With his father's smile lingering deep within his eyes,

I was lost in the rain, but your friendship led me to
Sunshine and whispered in my ear that it was
ok and For me to stop crying,

I know you're in a better place /but I needed you
In this place / to make this place a better place / and
Show our people how to escape these ghetto blues,
agony embeds it's self in our face.

So for now I'll throw my fist to the heavens
And give you dap,
        tattooing your name near my spine /
           remembering you had my back.

The scene replays, the crime / the bullet.
Poverty pumping through my veins,
eyes crying... thoughts raining,
they say the streets are watching, but do they
        Watch your back ?

Where the phrase keep it real... got me attending
A funeral, burying my man. . .what's real about that.

I had nothing to do with this poem.......
        My tears wrote it while I was lost in the rain,

CARDIAC

Paralyzed in non- belief,
How stupid was I ?
I now drop my heart on the paper
stabbing it with a pen,
Mixing blood with ink
Spilling and un concealing
naked thoughts,
Swimming in pools of no water.
Crushing my world,
Holding back tears that reveals
My weakness.
You said words with frostbitten languages
That hung me from your expressions.
My tears ran down my cheek,
falling off my jaw-
committing suicide on my shoes
as I exited the room.
With hurt being an understatement.
I was injured
With migraine heartaches.
As the "promise"
almost collapsed my senses.
For one split second
I felt the darkness of a hundred
Blind men sitting in a dark room,
Being abandoned by sight,
a hundred deaf men
yelling in sign language,

Wearing headphones on my hands,
middle finger music
With the bass up.
Escaped by the lullabies of togetherness,
A hundred scentless roses,
planted in a garden
that never felt the warmth of sunlight,
Neglected by the rain
That helps them grow,
the bitterness of a hundred forbidden spices,
Craving the sweetness
of honey covered thoughts,
That lost its taste between memories,
a hundred bullets piercing my soul,
Putting holes in a vest
I bought from love.
The pain administered a stroke
numbing my heart,
I prayed to hear the words
" I still love you "
Slither from her lips
So I could dive through rooms
catching them with my tongue,
And at that precise moment,
I lost the will to ever love again.

H E A R T B R E A K

I keep saying I'm not going to waist ink
On another piece of heartbroken poetry.
It should be a law
For heartbreak to be taught in school,
And if you don't experience heartbreak,
you can't get your degree
In knowing what love is.

It's been written that,
 time is the only thing to mend
A wounded heart,
that's bullshit !
Time splashed alcohol on mine,
The only thing that can heal a wounded heart
Is a piece of mind.

Take it from me,
I was a prince... I am now the artist
Formally known as Chris,
Cause with love comes lost of conciseness,
raping me with empty promises.

I keep saying I'm not going to waist ink
On another piece of heartbroken poetry.

Have you ever heard your soul cry ?
Well I've been lead to believe
That a man is not suppose to cry,

But what is a man to do
when his soul cries ?
And his eyes has no more tears to drown what
reality itself,
Is scared to swim in.

My last heartbreak I spoke to love,
And she told me,
The only way to heal a wounded heart
Was to have her,
And I need not seek her for she will come,
and only then,
would my fingers become numb,
Un-capable to write another heartbroken poem.

EXPRESSIONS

I never understood why people would look into my face,
And move their lips kind of like they were reading.
Strangers would sometimes hug me and say they understand.
A person once told me that
        power comes from your expressions.
Children would look at me saying letters, but too young
        To make out the words,
And when I was hiding something, my expressions would
        Be written in script.
But when in anger only certain expressions make sense,
        the rest were just mis spelled words.

                        A blind man once touched my face;
My skin formed pimples allowing him to read my
        thoughts in braille .
A person's life lies deep within their eyes,
        when age sets in, my wrinkles will form schematics,
Making it hard to read my facial poetry,
        you could find a complete novel in a person's eyes.
Just never underestimate what you might have missed,
        When you didn't read between the lines.

WHEN HOPE DIES

Once a good girl,
now scorned by the harsh world
Of weak men
with reputations of strong words.

She lies frozen in the cold weather,
Cause no one ever truly held her,
So she thinks she'll never find
Soothing arms of shelter.

This may sound odd but love has casualties,
prostitution,
suicide
and homosexuality's.

Now the phrases are: It's ok to be lesbian,
No good men
lots of good women,
And lots of absurdities spoon fed
To the ears of innocent children.

Fellas......... what have we done ?
A once good girl before the barrel of a gun,
Because she thought she found
...... the one.

How could we bring ourselves
to harm and to deceive,

The one in which we were taught,
nurtured and conceived,
And the twisted thing about it all is,
we fool ourselves to believe,
That with out a good black woman
We can truly achieve.

H   a   s   h   o   p   e
   d   i   e   d

Did we kill hope
and bury it deep inside,
And replace the words I'm sorry with
"Hey I tried".

I once knew a polished diamond
Told over and over again
That she was a cubic zirconia,
All because he was abandoned
and didn't want to be alone again
..... lose control again.
So he abused her beauty
destroyed her pride and ....
Lost control again.

She cries for no reason
and wonders why God
Doesn't answer her prayers.
She sits across the room
staring in the mirror,
Nonchalant to her own image,
Putting on make up

trying to create a new person.

She no longer cares,
she's alienated herself from feelings,
No longer believes in love.
Faith kept on leaving
So she stopped believing in......
Believing.

Bathroom door closed water hot
she feels cold inside,
Window open
you could hear the rain
Hit the puddles outside,
Wrist slit burgundy water...
Drifting out of consciousness; hope soon dies,

TEARS IN THE RAIN

Wandering the rain,
Camouflaged her tears,
Holding a baby in her arms
 wrapped in a blanket of
Motherly love.
Heart broken was I ,
wanting to hold her in my arms:
Cry on my shoulder my sweet,
All men aren't like that.
What did he do,
Put his hands on you ?
 Disrespect you ?
 If he said he loves you he lied,
All of these thoughts angered me
Ripping me out from the inside.
"I'm just trying to get home" she replied.
With clothes dripping wet
I opened the passenger side door of my ride.
Her eyes called my name;
 she didn't even know my name,
Overcasted by immense pain.
I stood broken hearted in the rain,
What could make a man
put his newborn out in the rain?
I couldn't fathom the music his insides played.
I couldn't grasp the method to his madness
 that gave me headaches when I envisioned his face ,
Making men look bad...

No, making black men look bad.
Mouth dry I lost all brotherly taste.

      Weeks later standing on a corner
Sunny day
but it rained on her skin,
I can't understand why women go back to these guys
The smell of feces thickens the air,
don't you see him surrounded by flies ?
And despite all my words
 to a sister giftwrapped
In brotherly tries,
This is a perfect example of what happens
When hope dies !

GHETTO GOSPEL

I cry blood for all my niggas who cant express themselves.
I'm the interpretation of concrete with R.I.P
graffiti hieroglyphics,
I'm the thesaurus of this concrete forest.
        I cried for the diallo verdict of innocent,
And then they wonder why my poetry's so militant.
        Them faggot ass cops need to walk the green mile,
In the court room crying when deep inside they smile.
        They better put out an a.p.b; all police beware
Of a poet like me,
All police beware cause poets don't sleep.
Yea I know ! the sight of his blood looked real sweet,
Don' sleep ya honor this shit is deep,
I felt his mothers tears when I seen her weep.
        The day of the hearing when justice for her son
Went wrong,
I seen a look in her face like no other.... this woman was
strong.
        As for Mr. Diallo, he played the man's role,
Fire scorched his insides and his heart got cold,
Thinking damn they done killed his body now they're
Aiming at his soul.
        I pantomimed and imagined myself on the block
Of the crime,
Guns were drawn ; them cops felt death in their palms,
 I wonder if they shouted nigga
        when they squinted their eyes And locked their arms,

They didn't get murder, reckless endangerment or man-
slaughter,
But this man- chris slaughter go plant 41 landmines,
One of the bullets missed and struck me in the shoulder,
Aiming 41 lines at blue uniforms,
putting a 3rd hole in that white cover,

Pretty soon we'll have to start writing our wills
When our bikes have three wheels,
Cause nowa dayz 6 year olds kills,
Cause nowa dayz dialing 911 kills,
Cause nowa dayz Giuliani kills,
Cause nowa dayz I cry blood in ghetto gospel, speaking in
smoke signals on roof tops when blood spills.

Hear My Cries at the Brooklyn Moon Café as trumpets blow in the background.
Brooklyn Moon Café, Fulton Street, Brooklyn, NY

HEAR MY CRIES

Lend me your eyes as I take you down the avenue of
    a young prophet's mind.
We're at war with those whom we pay to protect,
my pen screams & bleeds ink
    as I clutch my mental text,

Giuliani's gang wears colors of blue
    with eyes of suburban city thieves,
they throw gang signs like
    FREEZE....GIVE ME A REASON PLEASE.
......Death falls upon the ghetto,
illusions of Mary Jane hanging from trees,
she blows through an atmosphere of young thugs
praying to the ghost's of dead G's,
    with weed smoke surrounding their knees,

    ......Every day in the ghetto it rains,
contained to boroughs by slave style subway trains,
depending on metro cards turn the tracks
    into shackled chains.

The minds of young girls impregnated
by the persuasive words of hood legends incarcerated,
ancestral pigment makes us all related,
the color of god debated, the BOOK speaks the
    undeniable truth and
        YOU PEOPLE
          hate it !

these lyrics are "R" rated

RESTRICTION, ROTTEN,
    REDEMPTION OF RACIST RAIN,
you had shelter,
    so how the FUCK would you feel my pain,
I put all non believers to shame,
you accuse the streets
I say our parents are to be condemned,
       meanwhile.....

Wise words go un-heard as a homeless man whispers
to the concrete with his face to the curb,
He fought for this country,
he now speaks to birds as we toss change
    at what we perceive to be absurd.
He has the eyes of a vietnam veteran,
his wife abandoning him at war,
so he injected heroin in his malanin,
lying on corners w/ a sip of salvation left in his bottle

    So what's all this talk about
      freedom....freedom....free...dumb,
those who think they are free are dumb,
they pull me over
    aiming their guns calling me shit like
boy / son......these issues weigh a ton.

Don't be ignorant, white people don't run shit.
They just walk through an already written skit,
speaking from racist lips
    that crave to suck on a darklynippled tit.

I need ya'll to hear my cries,
  tissue can't eradicate my tears,
the cradle put a damper on my gums,
  forcing me to teethe off my surroundings.

I PLEDGE ALLEGIANCE TO THE FLAG
OF THESE FUCKED UP STATES OF AMERICA,
AND TO THE REDUNDANT,
WHICH ALWAYS STANDS,
SALVATION...BLACK IS GOD,
NOT INVISIBLE,
WITH NO LIBERTY
AND DEATH LISTS FOR ALL.

DEAR LOVE:

This letter will be thrown into the sea, hoping the water. Doesn't mix with tears written on these recycled trees. Every time I call you, the phone just seems to ring out, Sometimes I think you're screening your calls with lovers Id. You let me sip from your glass, but never to let me finish the drink. You blow smoke in my face whenever I get close enough to see your eyes. You give your cousin infatuation letters to give me, But before I could read them my tears smear the ink. My smile has become foreign to the rest of my expressions. I've become immune to pain, & I carry around an umbrella because I'm always expecting rainy days. I try to keep the word bitch out of my vocabulary, but every time I turn around female dogs with human faces are shit-ting on my emotions and pissing on my tree of rarities. I used chalk to write on darkness. Black ink just blends into my thoughts of the night when I speak to dreams. My pillow can no longer take the place of a warm soft body that I want to pull closer and closer with every inhale. You may not ever receive this letter unless you're swimming in the sea ,but maybe someone who knows you will find this letter washed upon the shore line.. So until I get a response........

HAIKU

Life is a bitch right ?
so then who fathered this shit
the one's we call bitch

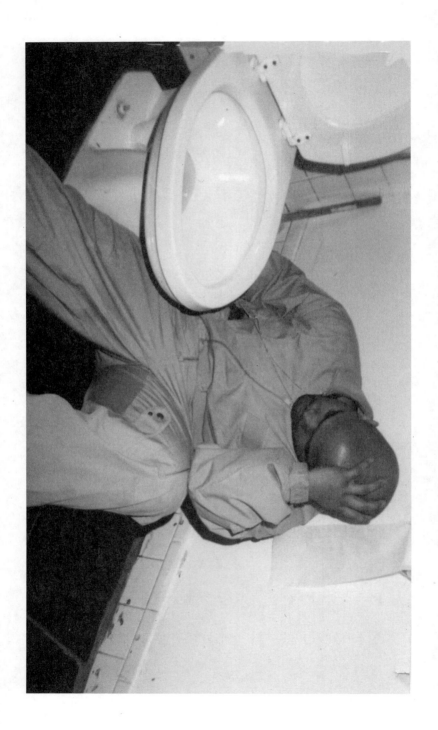

THE REALEST SHIT I EVER WROTE

S H E . H U R T . M E

She hurt me so bad my pride & my ego
had brawls & arguments in crowded places,

my pain would echo when I gazed into stranger's faces.
She strangled me with each breath she took.

I'd find myself mentally crying like my brain was sweating,
leaking commitment through faithful eyes,

tears escaped me running injured from
stares of disappointment.

C H R I S . S A Y . G O O D B Y E !

You got me acting out of my character,
talking to bed sheets, stealing kisses from old photos,
You hurt me with "fuck your feelings", "I don't cares"
and..."I love you".
I felt like a counterfeit dollar broken into fractured pennies,

The one I adored, hung my heart on the wall,
nailing it to the floor,
tension forcing oxygen from the room..... Damn MI Amour.

This Be The Realest Shit I Ever Wrote.

She had her hands around my throat, fighting for custody of
that three word quote.

She hurt me so bad I hailed a cab forgetting I had a car,
back seat to a stranger,
praying to a fictitious star.

This girl uttered crippling vocabulary that pierced my
sleep into zero hours,
reversing my hot baths to cold showers,
making my garden of love to dead flowers,
she had kool-aid cavities with a tongue gone sour.

Overflowing with her trust, making myself empty inside,
I Tried...and tried...and tried.. But her blatant eyes told
childish lies,
disguised in demeanors of smiles, my love you denied.

Who gave you the authority ? You signed the signature of
love, a forgery.

This Be The Realest Shit I Ever Wrote.

If this were winter and she were my coat,
I would freeze to death.

THIS POEM IS NOT A JOKE!!!!

I wouldn't wish this pain on my worst enemy,
and there's only one remedy.
make love mentally before physically,
and be connected spiritually.

T H E
U N T I T L E D

Fuck the moon, Fuck the stars, and Fuck the rain-
bows ....
You see cloudy days no longer matter, when I have sunshine
LYING BESIDE ME.

All this time I was fooled by
figures seen in deceitful mirrors,
I looking into your eyes,
seeing my reflection for the very first time.

Overwhelmed,
nervous symptoms,
I felt captured by your eye contact,
with stares bright enough to
leave shadows on the sun,
.... your eyes fucked with my mind.
You don't make any sense....
someone as beautiful as yourself ,
God must have just finished creating you
yesterday,
a thousand roses picked from heaven
had nothing on this woman

You can't be photographed,
seducing my complexities,
rendering me color blind,

.... you are the complexion of love.
I keep secrets from myself
that I can only remember
when I see you asleep,
and you whisper to me
in the languages of dreams.
.... I can smell you when I hold my breath,
I have sketches of you under my eyelids
that reminds me,
I've memorized the features of perfection.
Is that god I taste on your lips ?
Because if so......
What was that I tasted on your other lips ?
HEAVEN ?

That's why I say..........
Fuck the moon, Fuck the stars, and Fuck the rainbows,
because nothing else matters when I have sunshine
LYING BESIDE ME.

STAY. . . . .NO LEAVE

Give me my keys please,
       kissing the little one on the cheek,
       My once sugar coated freak
       360-ed to a bitter sweet,
       I think there's another man in my bed
       wrapped in my emotionally torn sheets,

I need you to go,
       my wants no longer controls
       the stress on my soul,
       my physical grows cold,
       I tried calling the cops
       but they couldn't arrest you
       for the felony of my heart you stole,

I don't want you to leave,
       But awakening in cold sweats
       making it hard for me to breath,
       envisioning another man climaxing with you,
       face dripping sweat between your knees...
       Makes me have needs, like these,

I can recall how your skin would glow
       when my hands embraced just above
       your eyebrow with an adoring touch,
       I now see that glow returning except
       ....it wasn't my touch,

Exposing vacant hugs,
making love to you, screaming my signature
on your dotted spine,
penetrating you in pools of perspiration,

What kept us together is
the caliber of a man that I am,
But GOD DAMN
How much shit do you think a good man
can possibly stand ?
Submerging deeper, deeper,
deeply immersed in love's quicksand,
With no one lending me their hand,
obliging to reassure coziness of dry land,

So therefore I want you to stay,

But I need you to leave,

So when you leave for work in the morning,
let the door slam lock, and leave your keys.

ALLEYCAT
(my death in harlem)

My pop's a wild cat, ran the streets since I was a kitten,
pushed from the garbage can early,
forced to be a ghetto street cat,
My mom's a sweet pussy taught me side street
and kept her tit in,
I studied slang & watched gun go from rod to burner to gat.

I tell tales of poverty, murder and every day life,
If the streets could talk
I'd be the tongue in the mouth of the savaged beast,
adultery, each borough I made my wife,
till death do us part or till the world becomes deceased.

I once jumped in a garage can and landed
on the bare chest of a new born child,
Results of a young girl in solitary
abandoned to be a single mom,
It was a little girl,
I licked her cold face but her warm heart
managed to let her smile,
I prayed, while quoting scriptures of my ghetto psalms,

I remember when T- Bone showered sha
with a silent blood-bath,
I knocked over some garbage
as soda bottles cracked and slightly rolled,
Fearing a hidden witness, he saw a black cat

and just laughed,
But had no idea I'm a feline with a human soul,

The perverted streets prey on a tight pussy and purring tits,
I lost one of my lives over a pussy with a nice tail,
Confronted in Harlem back to the wall two rocks
and a love sick pit,
I fought to my death on a bag of garbage
and blood on my nails.

THE 19th LETTER

If the good die young, I might die right now.
Balancing myself on tight ropes of wet thread,
falling next to what appeared to be me, lying in dirt dressed
up. . . AM I ALREADY DEAD ?
Sweat and hot tears burn my eyes, waking up silently
screaming words of no real meaning,
contemplating these thoughts beneath my breath.....I was
just dreaming.
On my way to the bathroom I stumbled across my
soul,
and he told me I wasn't dreaming,
he told me he was just looking for the definition of me.
He asked me did knowledge X life = existence, and if so
what times what equals eternity ?
He also stated that all the poetry I write is not mine,
he told me he borrowed them from a spiritual spoken word
reading
with JESUS, ALLAH and BUDDHA battling for skin tone.
BUT BEFORE I COULD ASK HIM WHO won........
He told me I was his 90th physical being and we
were all poets,
and I lose a piece of my soul every time I complete a poem,
and the only way to get that piece of my soul back was to
recite
a poem to a lost soul diving into the ocean of unconscious
demise.
He grabbed my ears and told me if I listened closely
enough,

I could hear screaming angels disguising themselves as home-
less people,
roaming the congested streets quoting lessons of life but no
one ever listens.
      And if I wanted to know the definition of myself,
I had to multiply mother times father to the square root of
poetry, and
divide it by the number of souls passing through me.
      I said "O.K. , if you know so much about me, why
when I cry my tears
fall toward my ears, even when standing vertically ?",he said
I do that
so you can hear all the bull shit you cry about.
And so that your tears can play ancient patterns on your ear
drum,
sampling Egyptian rhythms that are programmed in your
finger nails.
      You are the 19th letter, the one that starts the word
SEE,
you see only prophets can truly SEE, PROPHET-SEE!
      Slaughter is only reverse of what you're destined to
do,
forget yesterday and focus on the rest of today and pray you
see tomorrow.
Faith is something you buy with spirit,
and a pure soul is not something you borrow.

Smacking me he said, "love thy GOD before thy self and
love thy self before women,
 GOD can give you infinite sea, for women can only give
you a puddle to swim in."

Do the math he said, how many times have you run
from your reflection,
chasing shadows that prayed to see the joyous glare of light ?
a woman did that.
she had abortions on your thoughts yet...you still had
orgasms on her memories.
          you had miscarriages of faith cause you couldn't hold
the birth of bliss
in your spiritual womb.
crying tears that danced with the blues, making love to jazz,
in rhythmic sheets of
 of R & B that rapped over off beat melodies of your smile,
          "LISTEN TO ME," he yelled holding my face,
"this physical waste land can't comprehend the languages of
the spiritual world,
you have a gift, and when you are released, they will
acknowledge the poems
of
C H R I S   S L A U G H T E R "

FRIENDS

She was just my friend,
Actually friend was just a title I stumbled across
When trying to become her man,
            when she spoke of other men
My heart would skip beats
Do somersaults
 and perform sudden shifts,
Because I knew she was a present
 I just couldn't figure out how to
Unwrap my gift,
every time the words I love you slipped from my lips,
            Reality tightened its grip,
Because my ideal woman was so fine,
 she came with fine print,
            when ever walking on the streets
I would smell her scent
And loose common sense,
She was always singing
When waking through a neighborhood
In my mind,
            and if beauty is in the eye of the beholder
I beheld her so deep in my eyes,
she had an apartment just under my pupils,
            she was breath taken,
Oxygen mimicked her style when ever
I held her close enough

to smell the back of her neck,
       I found myself imprisoned in friendship
Wishing we were enemies in love,
Instead of exchanging sweat
And touching lips,
I kissed her fore head
 and gave her twenty second hugs,
       her waist line added intriguing melody
to my bass line,
 her voice was like the ocean meeting the shore line,
Damn ! she drove me crazy with that laugh of hers,
      I often choreographed
 how my tongue would dance between her knees
Play hide and go seek between her thighs,
I craved her like a table full of my mother's sweet
       potato pies,
But I was motionless in becoming
      more than just a friend,
I guess you can say
 she went to the highest bidder,
Which only made me quiver with bitter,
And I damn near lost my mind
When I heard he hit her,
He's the reason she refers to men as
 no good ass niggas,

I sometimes joked and would say
 "Watch, one day we're gonna get married",
And she would jokingly smack my arm and say
 "Stop playing",
But she had no idea that I was praying,

For the day she didn't smack my arm and say
"Stop playing."
As time went on,
I stopped asking her to marry me,
one knee,
Dark and crowded room, I asked her to
Be my friend forever.

A ROSE IN THE SNOW

I have menstrual cycles in my heart,
Because every month my chest bleeds,
Moods swinging
In a tired reoccurrence,
I hold the scorching taste of life
 in the back of vaguely
Understood relationships,
Overflowing with feelings
Of what I thought was love,
        a blind folded rose sways back and forth
Buried in snow that never melts,
The cold,
 its true means of shelter,
It never fully blossoms,
she fooled my fingertips
With the feelusion of a warm stem,
How was I to know it had frozen leaves
 with cold red petals,
That photographed winter
On all the seasons of the heart,
she lost a petal each time a hand attempted to
Remove her from the illusions of snow,
She only dreamt of sunshine,
But the cold ground shattered
All warm thoughts,
        the demeanor of this rose was so distinctive,
 every other flower swayed in the sun,
Shade found her in an open field,

I pulled her out of the snow
She brushed against my cheek
 turning my smile into a confused look
Of dejavu,
Swimming in a shallow ocean of regrets ,

PROSPECT PARK

She had a virgin mind to the city
with a love for the suburbs.

Never dealt with herbs with a body
full of unseen curves,

Forced to the city by destiny and
a slight touch of fate,

If stress was calories, sweetness
was 100 pounds over weight,

We cuddled on a bench one evening
in a quiet park,

We discussed us and sensitive
problems of the heart,

Just before we left, 5 words were
profoundly said to me,

On the 15th remember this date.
          "Promise Not To Hurt Me,"

DURING THE BLACKOUT

I firmly stand adjacent to reality with the past behind me,
Staring the future in the face with tears in my eyes,
  having holy wars in my mind, my ears bleeding,
 my first born's spirit held in the ink of my pen,
Repenting the sins of two souls in the words of one prayer,
Hidden in parables of street slang and ancient hand shakes,
  I walk around with dirty clothes and clean thoughts,
Fooling the eyes of intellects, camouflaging myself into
The scenery of the ghetto,
  I disappear in the crowd,
   tattooing tear drops of poetry
On the earlobes of newborns,
Erasing the scars on the naked eye exposing sinful behavior
To innocent pupils,
  I then blackout 20 stories
  below the subway basement,
I told stories on every story speaking calmly but
My heart was racing,
  where Dr. king and brother Malik wore black gloves,
And the phrase by any means became an expression,
And those who wore smiles became people of the past,
  muslims, israelites and black panthers formed as one,
And made crypts and bloods into a bed time story told to
Infants in the 21st century when they got caught
listening to rap music,
  Blackout... I was behind harriet escaping idumeans
Running through sewer like catacombs,
 I take the subway,
Just to mentally find my way home,

I found myself in the 70's, my pops wore a black fisted
comb,
Fast forward to the 80's ; no father figure, strong women
Held down a stable home,
     Black out... 2 /16 I fled into the world running from
the d.n.a of a sensitive style,
 loosing a fight that labeled me, semi-bastard child,
Endorsing my sanity on the backs of child support checks,
     Black out I wrote the remix to the ghetto streets,
I did windmills and back spins over break beats,
Revolutionary, militant poet lingo be what I speak,
     random thoughts weigh heavy on my mind,
Sometimes forget who I am,
     several personalities leave me signs,
     When I blackout jumping through portals in and
       out of time,

BROOKLYN STATE OF MIND

You can't travel trough my mind state,
You'll see signs that say next thought 10 miles and you
Only have two miles of gas,
so what do you do, you take a back street and run into
The eyes of a sober man with intoxicated thoughts and
weeded memories of being abandoned by life,
and for the first time in your life you looked winter
In the eyes and seen summer spring to the fall of poverty,
A success in this forsaken land I got to be,
So put your mind in neutral take off the condom cause
We about to fuck the world and commit sodomy,
Its time to say definite fuck the word probably,
We got our kids saying sick shit like mommy
Should've swallowed me,
Now walk down the street that separates
Bushwick and Bedsty
So follow me,
broadway a broad-way
where broads look the other way
And broads who went astray be making niggas pay,
just across the tracks one kid lost his toupee,
He was too late too- pay,
I'm from brooklyn,
a place where your block is tattooed
As an expression on your face,
And women are only attracted to dudes who been to jail,
Going to jail or back and forth to court fighting a case,
And if you feel out of place you need to get out of that
place,

I   G   N   O   R   A   N   C   E,
Negroes wanna be that italian in scarface,
Running down their nikees
       when Al Pacino ain't even running
The same race,
       you see around my way every one looks alike with
Down Syndrome,
They have the,
       wanna be down syndrome vacant inside with no
Address trying to find their way home,
       shit, I'm so blunt they want to smoke me,
Put fire to my flesh and I'll get the world high,
       Choke off my potency

       Brooklyn..... a place where thugs and intellects pass
notes,
 no one votes , former gangstas become old folks,
 children wear two jackets
       cause they can't afford winter coats,
And cancer got Giuliani by the balls
       while he got us by the throat,
       in Brooklyn we bring the art of war
         like Picaso & Sun Tzu,
Walk up in city hall strapped with grenades and guns drew,
Its a time to kill like Sam Jack, fuck what you think,
I'm an endangered species becoming extinct,
Pretty soon they'll be wearing black skin like mink,
Line for line my soul speaks through black ink,
       I put an order of protection out on myself,
lost my voice
And started writing death threats to red necks,
       I be the spook who sat by the door,

Naked, soaked in the blood of Asata Shakur with my boy's
name
Tattooed on my spine, clutching my self published tears,
         I believe it was 2Pac that said
"Pussy, Paper, Poetry, Power and Pistols",
Around my way every one has tattoos across their skin tissue,
 those are the targets for the bullets not to miss you,
No two blocks are identical,
 bullets whistle tearing through bone gristle,
..........." yo Ty I miss you "
A Brooklyn state of mind ; a place you can't travel through.

I THOUGHT I WAS OVER YOU

Must this withered reality continue to drown me in its
nightmares of unhappiness.
You were gone,
you said what you had to say
speaking into the night like shadows fading into darkness.
Is this some type of game you play
  toying and teasing my emotions,
I thought you were gone.
 Was I fooling myself locking them in the back room,
in the back of the closet,
 in the back of my mind,
in the back of my....
I thought I was over you.
Who gave you permission to moon walk back into my life
  breakdancing on my contradictions ?
Making me look fool
in front of my goddess I call poetry.
I cried on her shoulder, promising to never mention your
name,
crushing my pride,
tossing my feelings into the cosmos,
disregarding the tears I once wiped from your cheek.
You were a lost soul
 roaming the city streets shivering cold,
in search of a spirit sheltered in love
 surrounded by innocence.
Am I a fiend for pain ?
smoking heartbreak

blowing clouds of lonely nights from my nose.
No one knows how much pain I smoke
in privacy when the doors are closed,
        I just dose...
sitting in a dark corner naked
cause I can still smell your scent in my clothes.
I thought I was over you......
        For the sake of love I sacrificed my pride and lost all
H A P P I N E S S,
wrapped in sheets
that still seem to have your scent.
I take showers in your old bath water
  to feel the memories of minutes before
 when you clutched the sheets, shaking with lust and love
cascading in your eyes
Photos just ache the left side of my chest,
 I catch headaches trying to spell your name
cause the letters don't exist yet.
I lie down on top of memories
cause I don't understand love yet.
I walk down the roads of life
 balancing my self on the yellow lines,
being torn apart by two directions, trying to decipher in
decisiveness,
  I G U E S S I ' M N O T O V E R Y O U !

STEP FORWARD STEP BEHIND

My people we're not living well,
only you I tell we're destined in life to a prison cell,
I hold my head and start to rebel, but no one hears me yell,
My tears fall into a bottomless well where judges deny
me bail and..... sentence me to this Ghetto Hell.
Having no rights makes me left handed to devilish needs,
Stress craves itself in cigarette butts and marijuana trees,
P   L   E   A   S   E !!
wear a condom if you can't support more seeds.
Hypocrites wear fashionable garments trying to fake it,
But it's a cold world and I lie naked, clothed in stolen pig-
ments of hatred.
I bless open mic's to repent and stay sane,
But as soon as I step outside tornado storms or rain, turn to
Blood from historic torture of our people brutally slain.
Negro ink on caucasian paper
Creating inter-racial lyrics of a lost race.
KKK marching in Manhattan, lynching the millennium
historical slaps in the face
We talk of million man marches, Harlem youth lynchings,
Washington's march of a million women,
But what is the use if we leave and start sinning ?
 Stop Blaming slavery for your unemployed laziness,
the shackles are off now but mental imprisonment got me
pissed,
COPS, THE MEDIA, POLITICIANS, hear this; "Take US
OFF OF YOUR DEATH LIST".
I swing words tormenting blue suits, this time I won't miss,

Evil spirits taunt me telling me I'm gonna die
A poetic myth, that I will never get to use this gift,
But etched on my soul reads eternity on my capability's width.
My people I know you hear a lot of anger,
And who is this prophetic stranger
          warning me of an obvious danger ,
But if it is so obvious, why do we continue killing
Self determination, like babies aborted with coat hangers ?
It's not about the red pill or the blue pill,
my matrix consists of five boroughs, and its kill or be killed,
                    Strong wills are assassinated by
blue clothes and gold shields,   Hiding in the darkness of
that shit they call the law.

They use authority escaping explanation for this modern day segregation,
On this modern day plantation,
Well... This is my modern day translation.
While they worry about the skin surrounding our bones,
AND the texture of hair caught up in my comb,
AND how you try to duplicate us NIGGAS using the sun to clone our skin tone,
          ONLY 144,000 GO GET HOME,
          ONLY 144,000 GO GET HOME,

HAIKU

Writing from the heart
some may not understand
cause they have no heart

FROM THE HEART TO MY ESSENCE

Hey baby ! me and mommy wasn't getting along
so I had to........ move along.
It tears me up on the inside just to know
You're not biologically mine,
I often stay up nights composing my thoughts
Into tear jerking heart wrenching lines.
Your eyes alone stabs me, awakening,
hearing your cries in the midst of the night,
I wish you were a product of my sperm
And came from my vine of life.
Your father treated mommy like hell
When you were in her womb of life,
I wish I could've given her heaven
and asked her to be my wife
he may be your father but I'm your daddy.
You see, you and I have something strong,
Something he can't possibly understand.
I'd give you one side of my ribs just to show him
The definition of what it is to be a man.
By the time you're old enough to comprehend
And acknowledge these words.
Do me a favor,
Hug me
And let me know my tears
Didn't go unheard.
Mommy does a good job raising you,
She's perhaps the strongest woman
I've ever had, And trust me

I know what its like to be raised without a dad
        my mommy was alone
I had only two shoulders to cry on,
And being a little girl,
 you need a daddy to rely on.
          Your pain is my pain
          When life tends to do you harm,
Forever my baby,
My sunshine,
 my essence
.....my good luck charm,

I'VE MOVED ON

I walked in the room of my heart where you once lived,
Vacant memories paint the wall black so that the shadows
Of my past aren't noticed,

      wallpaper covers fist marks of anger, trademarks
Of my loneliness when you left,
Translucent to the mutters of deceit.

      I've moved on .... I have a new home.
My house is furnished with love, painted with joy, and shel-
tered
With happiness,
Smiles and laughter takes the place of light bulbs.
My sun continuously shines indoors.

      I keep shades on my window of heart to prevent
Darkness from lurking in like once before,
Camouflaging itself with the evening.
E   v   i   c   t   e   d! !
Find a new heart in which to live, feelings are gone,
Just something brief to let you know ...... "I've moved on".

ANGELS

Was I just a fall fling ?

A young thing,

Lost in the melody of how you sing,

Teasing my eyes flashing only one wing,

It took a prince to show a queen she had no king,

You now move closer to that white dress and ring,

You were treated like winter with a heart of spring,

Couldn't carry tears had nothing but love to bring,

Hey bright eyes I love you still

Cunning and stunning from now until,

Wish you could touch my eyes and see how I feel,

Read my poems and feel just how real,

I'd be injured if love could kill,

Just something simple to let you know.....

When we were in love time stood still

AMERICA OFF LINE
www.lights out.com

Computer programmers hack their
way into my hard drive.
Anti-virus programs no longer prevent
diseases corrupting
My three and a half floppy disk of
thoughts.
Putting bars on my windows with 2000
mega bites of lost
Memories floating in my 12 by 8 feet
of cyber space.

They sell phones, they sell
phones....cell phones, brain cancer,
Listen to the computerized moans,
They take the place of hormones,
hormones...........whores moan,
Hearts of stone, she now has a degree
in being all alone.
She was replaced by a computerized
street walking clone.
Boot legging pussy over cd rom, std
unknown.
Sexual stimulation through the use of
head phones, leaving brains exposed.

Cross out freedom of speech, they
can e-mail you racism, child
pornography, information to leave you
brain dead.
Computers program idiot-ologys in our
head.
13 legged spiders trap you in the
nation wide web.
Nation wide we re caught up

in a world wide web.

        Be careful what you download when
your drive is hard.
You don t come with a rebootable disc
when times get hard,
Computer keys don t fit in doors that
are financially scared,

        we stomp roaches and trap mice
when a double click of the mouse can
get you evicted from your house, thrown
in jail,
Identity erased, no support for your
kids and spouse.

        Lost tribes of the ghetto enter
the nigga net.
Rewinding the Matrix trying to find
proof.
Open your window, sit on the roof and
observe what you ve
Grown addicted to.
Illusions of false profits are twisting
the truth.

        Genetic engineering smearing
traits from our make up.
D.N.A technology never sleeps,
wake..up,
america is off line, out of line, out
of their conscious state of minds,
Computers will decide if you finish
these lines.
                www.lights out.com

SURVIVE TO DIE

Every day the ghetto gives birth, and the pain is felt up and down the traverse and decaying streets. prostitution and betrayal exists in a chain- like pattern, so that infants and drug lords coexist to eat,

Murals of loved ones skillfully articulated to remind and mourn past souls now gone, while crackheads & dope fiends trade their lives like gold and jewels now pawned,

Questions of their existence remind us of what not to become, my question was a millionaire addicted to drugs or an educated bum?

Ponder, don't pick the shoes in which you walk because of style or cost, pick the shoes that are scuffed and run down with laces now lost,

Or perhaps look at a woman compared to expensive rubies yet treated as your average stone, but the distress of life became unbearable to the point of her taking her own,

Then look at a shorty, his life is subject to downfall as I schooled the young one, but he just smirked, shrugged his shoulders, and clutched his hand gun,

Months later his body jerked, fighting death but his effort in life was now done, as his spirit left his body he could see, his girl, another man, and what seemed to be the smoke from his own gun.

CANCEROUS WORDS

Here I lay,
being fed from a bag, tubes through my chest,
are there angels where I'm going,
and peace where I'll rest ?

The pain that I feel stabbing me, tied up,
assassinating my soul
I shiver as I visualize tears of loved ones as my body lies cold.
weaving through consciousness I feel lonely, mother's
youngest child,
My moms remains strong, but emptiness jackets her
stable yet diluted smile.
I'm blessed, a mom's who praises GOD, I feel her when she
prays hard ,
 back in consciousness, seeing white walls with GET WELL
cards.
I can't believe I'm having these cancerous - chemotherapy -
hair thinning thoughts,
It's like I went to trial and was sentenced to death
by the highest possible courts.
Its funny how I thought I found my soul mate,
but when my inner fire started to burn, she ... she hit the fire
escape
instead of being my water to ease my fate.
Under my breath I whispered "why" through a tube,
wrinkling my bed sheets holding them ever so tightly,
I then shamed myself, for questioning THE DOINGS OF
THE ALL MIGHTY.

I feel my veins are pumping death and my white blood cells
were taken by demons,
I'm asking questions, indirect answers and begging
for reasons.
I'm young, I was strong, I was supposed to live long,
I chose paths of right not wrong,
so why do I hear angels playing harps and singing such
relaxing songs,
Its unfair, its unfair I say ....I'm loosing my hair,
all these bags connected to my veins and I can't, I can't
think clear,
I'm losing my mind in This Cancerous Atmosphere.
My healthy features evaporated into the hospital air.
I'm broken, shattered into fragments of a confused spirit
inside,
I read my bible and yet I still have whys?whys?and more
whys?
A confused flurry of tears, overcasts and blankets the
loudness of my cries.
I black out, start talking to GOD
but then open my eyes to the darkness of a cold room,
I cry and wish I could return to the essence of my mothers
womb.

A SUICIDE NOTE

Find me in a mental institution,
looking for sanity in the arms of staight jackets.
The world falling to pieces with the solution
hidden in the canes of senior citizens,
ignorance climaxing in young hanicapped thinkers
giving birth to special ed prodigies.
Trans-parents reversing labor pains into monthly
abortion visits,
holding cemetaries in her pelvic area.
Her mother's voice incarserated in her head,
blaming her father for getting her aroused
in a dark hallway fifteen years ago,
and made her
photographing womanhood in the eyes of
a young girl pushing a baby carriage,
blaming her mother for developing the film.

UMBILICAL SLANG

Initiated in lust,
born and premised into sin,
Be an addict for my writing, rubber band your vein,
And syringe my heart through the eyes of abortion eluded
men.
Perplexing how we learn from embryo
Until we die,
But then move backward from final breath to first cry.
My deepest conversation ever was with mom's,
I spoke through umbilical,
abortion carved on my neck,
Chest and arms.
I designed works of art, and composed heartfelt
words
Onto the vaginal wall,
Mommy stressed, arguing, I managed to make out
2 words,
Abortion call.
G.y.n. "Ma don't do this",
sitting knee to chin,
Too young.....
Exited the same door she walked in,
I knew there was a reason why I'd walk into clinics and the
Air gets thin.
Mommy don't cry,
I can sense your tears,
Beautiful , young, innocent to rigorous predicaments,

I wish you were round enough
 to rub your belly and feel my feet,
We're all we have... talk to me.

> *I'm too young ,*
> *His words forced me to be a woman,*
> *I opened my legs for the wrong reasons,*
> *Now you're coming.*
> *Blinded and side tracked into responsibility,*
> " ma... don't get rid of me",
> *I have to ,*
> *With you here I wont be able to*
> *... you know... live.*
> *Look at me , a teenager, I have nothing to give,*
> But wouldn't you want hear my first words,
> Make sure I don't fall in my first attempts to walk,

There was silence, no response,

I looked to a higher power to have a talk.
He told me to seek the elder by the name of Josephine,
He said your grand ma will raise you,
Mommys only in her teens.

MONOLOGUES

NO ONE UNDERSTANDS

Where's my father, where's my brothers, where the
hell is my daughter's father? Where are all the positive males
In my life? Do I even know how to love a man?
No one understands.....life stresses me out forcing
Issues of love, what is love? Whatever it is I know I
Have it for my essence....the essence of me!
Why.....why can't I be closer to my mother? I love her,
In life's cold weather why cant she be my comforted
Cover? No one understands me, maybe...maybe
That's why I can't express my self cause I'm scared
That no one will understand. I been through hell
And back and the only one that stood beside me
Was my baby....lord knows how much I love my baby.
I don't know how to express my feelings,
Because...because....I don't know why, maybe ...maybe
Because I never been taught how...I never been
Taught how! I wish I had a daddy, one I could hug,
Talk to, and get advice about life.
(Essence..essence come give mommy a hug).
I work hard, struggling to be a good mother,
Which I am. I wake up early every morning getting
You and I ready. I need a break, I need a vacation.
I love my daughter but I need time away,
No one understands...I want to be happy,
I want to smile more, I want to be loved, I want to...
What am I doing wrong, am I doing anything wrong?
Will I ever be happy? Will I ever find someone that
Loves me, someone that I love intuitively, someone

That smile has me looking forward to kissing...
I have a good heart but....do I let anyone know
That its there? Do I give them a chance to try
And understand?

Written through;

Hope

I AM CHANGING

Once again my talent has gone unnoticed,
I.... I break my neck trying to please others
When I'm not even pleased with myself... I need a change,
First I need to define what change is.
Is change something you get after you break a dollar,
Or is it something you get after you break ... your spirit ?
I've swam through an ocean of friends and walked a mile
In a pair of shoes that are too small for my feet.
Look at me ... look at me ... if I am so beautiful, why is it
that
My attitude has threathened all happy expressions ?
And ...... I don't know how much longer I'll be able to toler-
ate
The reflection of my own soul,
(dropping to your knees) " oh please lord please .... re-
release
Me from this prison created by no one other than myself,
Where shackles of change, shackles of .... change ... has-has
Blinded me to my own lies ",
but what is it that rests underneath lies....
Maybe some day I'll find the truth about a word that has
people
Digging in their pockets, screaming the word change
but.......
They have no sense,
 screaming the word, change,
But they have no cents,
.... I don't want to be alone anymore,

I once lost my mind and found a piece of it on my knees
(pause)
Talking to god, I rose to my feet, stood in the mirror
And began to sing to myself (song I am changing).